Author's Preface

Over the past ten years of working in children's ministry, I have learned that craft activities are very useful tools for effectively conveying the Bible. As I naturally accumulated content, I wanted to help church school teachers and missionaries who might have similar concerns. I believe that the greatest gift for children in mission fields is the Gospel. I hope that children can understand the Gospel in a more fun and meaningful way, so I chose a theme related to the Gospel.

Considering the unique environment of mission fields, I structured it to use minimal materials. I expressed the content in English, Korean, and pictures, so I believe it can overcome language barriers. Throughout the process of creating this book, I imagined children discovering God's love and being happy. I hope that Jesus becomes the greatest gift for them. I wish this can be helpful for Sunday schools and missionaries who have difficulty finding christian activities. *"You are Awesome!"*

지금까지 어린이 사역을 10여년간 하면서 크래프트 활동이 말씀을 효과적으로 전달하는데 아주 유용한 도구가 된다는 것을 알게 되었습니다. 자연스럽게 컨텐츠가 쌓이면서 비슷한 고민을 하고 있을 교회학교 선생님들, 해외 선교사님들에게 도움을 드리고 싶었습니다. 특별히 선교지에 있는 아이들에게 가장 큰 선물은 "복음"이 아닐까 싶습니다. 아이들이 좀 더 재미있고 의미있게 복음을 이해할 수 있기를 소망하며 복음에 관한 주제를 정했습니다.

선교지라는 독특한 현장을 생각하고 최소한의 재료만 사용할 수 있도록 구성했으며, 영어와 한글 그리고 그림으로 본문의 내용들을 표현했기에 언어의 어려움을 넘어설 수 있으리라 생각합니다. 저는 이 책을 만드는 내내 아이들이 하나님의 사랑을 발견하며 행복하고 즐거워하는 모습을 상상했습니다. 그들에게 예수님이 최고의 선물이 되었으면 좋겠습니다. 고군분투하고 계시는 한국의 교회학교와 선교현장에 계신 사역자들에게 도움이 되기를 소망하며, *"You are Awesome!"*

Kimberly Saem 김벌리쌤

CONTENTS

How To Use 4

What You Need 5

All About Me .... 6·7

1. God Made Everything 8
하나님이 모든 것을 만드셨어요

2. Sin came into the world 14
세상에 죄가 들어 왔어요

3. God Sent Jesus 16
예수님을 보내셨어요

4. Jesus Died 20
예수님이 죽으셨어요

5. Jesus is Alive 24
예수님이 살아나셨어요

English Virson C E V
한글성경 새번역

6. We Received a New Life 28
새생명을 얻었어요

7. We are Saved 32
우리가 구원 받았어요

8. You are Awesome 36
너는 정말 멋져

9. Jesus Always Lives for You 40
예수님은 항상 우리와 함께 하세요

Sharing the Sweet Message 44
달콤한 복음을 전해요

Memory Card Matching Game 49
메모리 게임

I am a Child of God 53
나는 하나님의 자녀입니다 (증명서)

Answers 정답 .... 55·56

HOW TO USE

All About Me This activity is for yourself to introduce you to your new friends. 이 활동은 새로운 친구들에게 나를 소개하는 활동입니다.

Bible Story, Memory Verse This memory verse holds the topic of the activity. The memory verse is important so read it many times to memorize it. 주제가 담겨있는 성경 본문과 암송 말씀입니다. 중요한 말씀이니 반복하여 외우도록 합니다.

My Works The instructions are simple and easy to follow. The activity helps you remember the word of God. 만들기를 통해 말씀을 기억하는 데 도움을 주는 활동입니다. 만드는 순서는 간단하고 따라 하기 쉽습니다.

Fun Activity This is an activity page that is fun. This page can be used for students who have finished other activities early. 재미를 더한 학습지 형식의 활동지입니다. 만들기를 먼저 끝낸 친구들이 기다려 주는 시간에 활용하면 좋습니다.

Sharing the Sweet Message Practice spreading the Gospel with this activity. 말씀을 따라 적용할 수 있는 내용을 포함하고 있습니다.

Memory Card Matching Game A memory game to find same words. You can use two sets to play with more friends. 같은 단어를 찾는 메모리 게임입니다. 친구들과 오려 2세트로 진행 할 수도 있습니다.

I am a Child of God (Certificate)
You can make this to hold your identity close to you. Write your name on the certificate. Bless each other and do not forget the joy of being a child of God. 하나님의 자녀라는 정체성을 품고 갈 수 있도록 증명서를 만들 수 있습니다. 증명서에 이름을 적고 서로 축복하고, 하나님의 자녀된 기쁨을 기억할 수 있습니다.

What You Need

* Teachers are requested to be careful when using craft knives as it may be dangerous for children.
* 커터 칼 사용 시 어린이들에게 위험할 수 있으니, 선생님들은 주의를 기울여주시길 바랍니다.

1 God Made Everything
하나님이 모든 것을 만드셨어요

Bible Story — Genesis 1:1-28

By creating the earth, God showed us His love and power. He made a wonderful world for us. The One who made the earth made me.

하나님은 세상을 만드시고 그분의 사랑과 능력을 보여주셨어요. 하나님은 우리에게 멋진 세상을 주셨어요. 그 하나님은 나를 만드신 창조주세요.

Memory Verse

Genesis 1:1

In the beginning God created the heavens and the earth.

태초에 하나님이 천지를 창조하셨다.
[창세기 1:1]

How to Make

❶ Color the picture and color the person to look like yourself.

❷ Cut the picture and all lines with a knife.
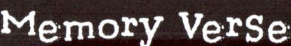

❸ Put the person into the center slit.
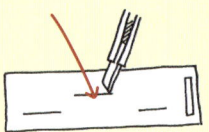

❹ Fold in opposite directions.

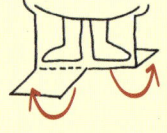

❺ Glue the flaps at the bottom.

❻ Fold and glue the flap down.
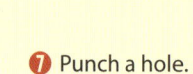

❼ Punch a hole.

❽ Bend and glue them on both sides.

❾ Insert a string into the hole and tie a knot.

❿ Insert the pictures into the slits.

WHAT YOU NEED
coloring tools
scissors
glue
string
craft knife
scissors

CUT
FOLD

GLUE

GLUE

GLUE

GLUE

Light

Darkness

Fun Activity

Forest Animals
Find 10 Differences

Answer 55p

2. Sin came into the world
세상의 죄가 들어 왔어요

Bible Story — Genesis 1:1 -28

Sin entered us from Adam and Eve. We did things that made God not happy, so we cannot be free from sin. We are far from God.

아담과 하와로부터 우리에게 죄가 들어왔어요. 우리는 하나님이 기뻐하시지 않는 일을 했고, 죄로부터 자유로울 수 없어요. 그리고 우리는 하나님으로부터 멀어졌어요.

Memory Verse

Romans 3:23

All of us have sinned and fallen short of God's glory.

모든 사람이 죄를 범하였습니다. 그래서 사람은 하나님의 영광에 못 미치는 처지에 놓여 있습니다.
[로마서 3:23]

Write down your sins on the handcuffs.

My Works

Chain of Sin

How to Make

WHAT YOU NEED
aluminium foil
scissors
6 paper rings
1 toilet paper tube

1. Cut the tube vertically.
2. Cut it in half horizontally.
3. Wrap the tubes with aluminium foil.
4. Punch a hole.
5. Connect the cuffs with paper rings.

3 God Sent Jesus
예수님을 보내셨어요

Bible Story — Matthew 28:1-10

God loves us, so he sent Jesus. Jesus is God's son. Jesus told us about heaven. We celebrate the day of His coming on Christmas.

하나님은 우리를 사랑하세요. 그래서 예수님을 보내셨어요. 예수님은 하나님의 아들이시고, 천국을 우리에게 알려주셨어요. 예수님이 오신 날을 기념하기 위해 우리는 크리스마스를 보내요

Memory Verse

Luke 2:11

This very day in King David's hometown a Savior was born for you. He is Christ the Lord.

오늘 다윗의 동네에서 너희에게 구주가 나셨으니, 그는 곧 그리스도 주님이시다. [누가복음 2:11]

How to Make

1. Color and cut out the picture.
2. Fold along the dotted lines.

WHAT YOU NEED
- coloring tools
- scissors
- glue
- 1 string
- easter grass
- tissue
- 2 colored craft sticks
- tape
- 1 (30mm) styrofoam ball

3. Glue both sides.
4. Tape craft sticks onto the roof.
5. Glue the star on the top of roof.
6. Draw a face on the styrofoam ball.

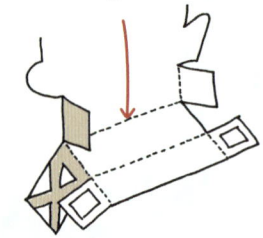

7. Lay the parts in this order: grass - face - tissue.
8. Tape a string onto the back.

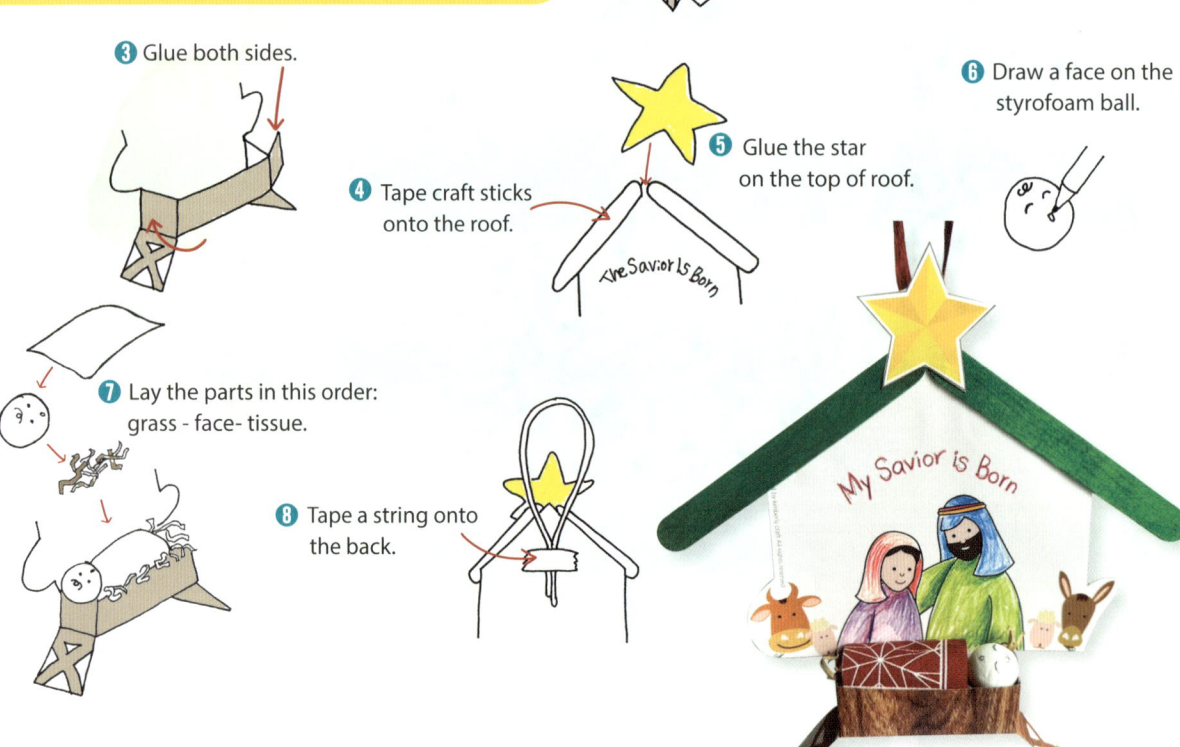

My Works
Savior Hanger

Fun Activity

Our King

Find the correct picture and write the number.

1.
2.
3.
4.
5.
6.
7.
8.
9.
10.

Answer 55p

4 JESUS Died
예수님이 죽으셨어요

Bible Story — Mark 15:22-25

Sin made us far from God. The result of sin is death. To solve this Jesus died. We can go closer to God thanks to his sacrifice.

죄는 하나님과 인간을 멀어지게 했어요. 죄의 결과는 죽음이기 때문에, 죄의 문제를 해결하기 위해 예수님이 죽으셨어요. 예수님 덕분에 우리는 하나님께 나아갈 수 있게 되었어요.

How to Make

WHAT YOU NEED
coloring tools
scissors
fastener
hole puncher
craft knife

1. Color and cut out the cross.
2. Cut the line with a knife.
3. Fold along the lines.
4. Glue.
5. Punch a hole.
6. Insert the fastener through the holes.
7. Insert the cross into the slit.

Memory Verse

Romans 5:8

But God showed how much he loved us by having Christ die for us, even though we were sinful

우리가 아직 죄인이었을 때에, 그리스도께서 우리를 위하여 죽으셨습니다. 이리하여 하나님께서는 우리들에 대한 자기의 사랑을 실증하셨습니다. [로마서 5:8]

Fun Activity

Cross Maze

Find your way to God.

Start

Answer 55p

4 JESUS is Alive
예수님이 다시 사셨어요

How to Make

Bible Story — Matthew 28:1-10

Jesus died on the cross and rose back to life. His grave was empty. Whoever believes in Jesus will have eternal life.

예수님은 십자가에서 죽으셨고 다시 사셨어요. 예수님이 죽은 무덤은 비어 있었어요. 예수님을 믿는 사람은 죽지 않고 부활할 수 있어요.

WHAT YOU NEED
- coloring tools
- scissors
- glue
- cotton
- paper cup
- pipe cleaner
- tape
- 2 wooden sticks

❶ Color in and cut out the pictures.

❷ Tie the middle of the cross with the pipe cleaner.

❸ Glue cotton onto the clouds.

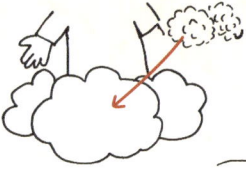

❹ Cut out the circle.

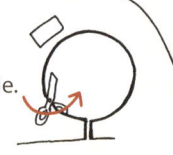

❺ Cut the top of the cup as shown and fold it out.

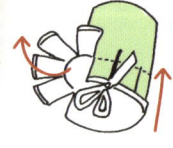

Memory Verse

John 11:25

Jesus then said, "I am the one who raises the dead to life! Everyone who has faith in me will live, even if they die.

나는 부활이요 생명이니, 나를 믿는 사람은 죽어도 살고, [요한복음 11:25]

❻ Tape the cross onto the back.

❼ Tape the paper cup onto the back of the circle.

❽ Glue the stone door onto the marked spot.

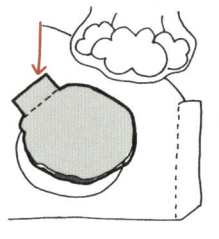

❾ Glue Jesus to the top of the empty tomb.

Fun Activity

My Jesus

Two pictures are the same. Find and circle them.

Answer 55p

6 We Received a New Life
새로운 삶을 얻었어요

Bible Story — John 1:1-12

Our sins are gone thanks to Jesus. He made us clean. Whoever believes in Jesus becomes a child of God and has a new life.

우리의 죄는 예수님을 믿고 깨끗해졌어요. 누구나 예수님을 믿으면 하나님의 자녀가 되고, 새로운 삶을 살 수 있어요.

Memory Verse

2 Corinthians 5:17

Anyone who belongs to Christ is a new person. The past is forgotten, and everything is new.

누구든지 그리스도 안에 있으면, 그는 새로운 피조물입니다. 옛 것은 지나갔습니다. 보십시오, 새 것이 되었습니다. [고린도후서 5:17]

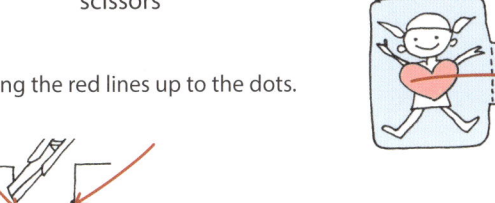

How to Make

WHAT YOU NEED
craft knife
scissors

❸ Insert it through the cuts.

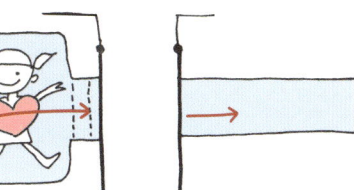

❺ Pull it out.

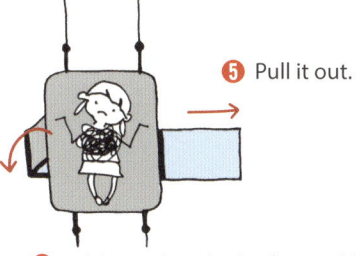

❶ Cut along the red lines up to the dots.

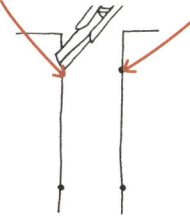

❹ Fold it so that the back is visible.

❷ Fold along the dotted lines.

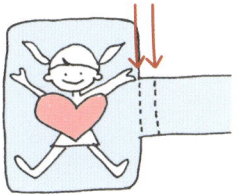

My Works

Washed Away

——————— CUT
- - - - - - - FOLD

29

Fun Activity

WORD SEARCH

Find words and Cicle each word. ↓ → ← ↘

r	e	l	p	r	o	m	i	s	e
g	e	k	a	t	s	i	m	p	s
o	n	s	y	r	o	l	g	c	a
s	i	n	u	f	a	i	m	r	l
p	l	a	c	r	o	s	s	o	v
e	u	t	o	e	r	g	o	d	a
l	a	n	r	e	t	e	z	n	t
i	o	f	a	i	t	h	c	j	i
f	e	v	i	l	a	b	e	t	o
e	d	j	e	s	u	s	m	k	n

Jesus God resurrect
glory sin promise
life love eternal
gospel alive salvation
cross faith free

 Answer 56p

Jesus:예수님/ God:하나님/ resurrect:부활하다/ mistake:잘못/ sin:죄/ promise:약속/ life:삶,생명/ love:사랑/ eternal:영원한/
gospel:복음/ alive:살아있는/ salvation:구원/ cross:십자가/ faith:믿음/ free:자유스러운

7

We are Saved
우리를 구해 주셨어요

Bible Story
Matthew 18:12-14

When we believe what Jesus has done for us, we get a new life. He saved us from sin.

예수님이 우리를 위해 하신 일을 믿으면 우리는 구원을 선물로 받을 수 있어요. 예수님은 우리를 죄로부터 구해주셨어요

Memory Verse

Romans 8:2

The Holy Spirit will give you life that comes from Christ Jesus and will set you free from sin and death.

그리스도 예수 안에서 생명을 누리게 하는 성령의 법이 당신을 죄와 죽음의 법에서 해방하여 주었기 때문입니다. [로마서 8:2]

How to Make

WHAT YOU NEED
- coloring tools
- scissors
- 1 paper cup
- hole puncher
- double-sided tape
- glue
- 1 string
- 1 bead

❶ Color and cut out the picture.

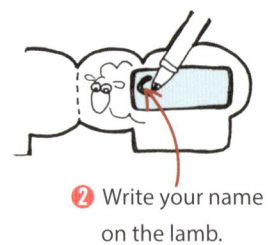

❷ Write your name on the lamb.

❸ Tape the string inside the lambs. and glue together.

❹ Glue "sin and death" onto the cup.

❺ Squeeze the cup.

❻ Punch a hole.

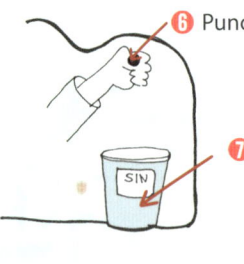

❼ Tape the cup with double-sided tape.

❽ Insert the string through the hole.

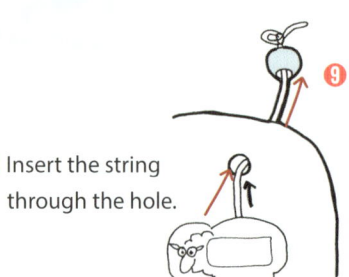

❾ Attach a bead to the end by tying a knot.

My WORKS

Jesus Saved Me

8 You Are Awesome

너는 정말 멋져

Bible Story — 2 Timothy 2:20-21

God loves us just as we are. We are special and valuable. We are God's masterpiece.

하나님은 우리의 모습 그대로를 사랑하세요. 우리는 정말 특별하고 소중해요. 우리는 하나님의 작품이에요.

Memory Verse

Zephaniah 3:17

"The Lord your God wins victory after victory and is always with you. He celebrates and sings because of you, and he will refresh your life with his love."

주 너의 하나님이 너와 함께 계신다. 구원을 베푸실 전능하신 하나님이시다. 너를 보고서 기뻐하고 반기시고, 너를 사랑으로 새롭게 해주시고 너를 보고서 노래하며 기뻐하실 것이다.
[스바냐 3:17]

How to Make

WHAT YOU NEED
coloring tools
scissors
string
hole puncher

1. Color and cut out the picture.
2. Fold the petals along the dotted line. 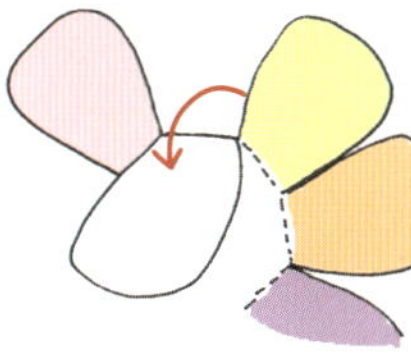
3. Roll up the petals. 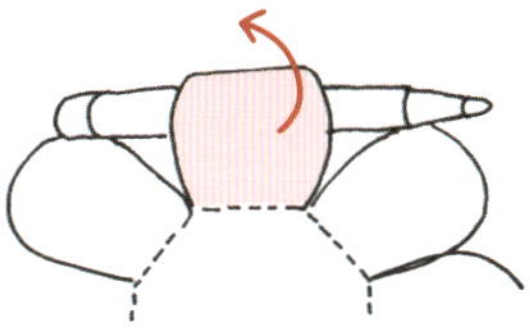
4. Punch a hole and tie a string through it.

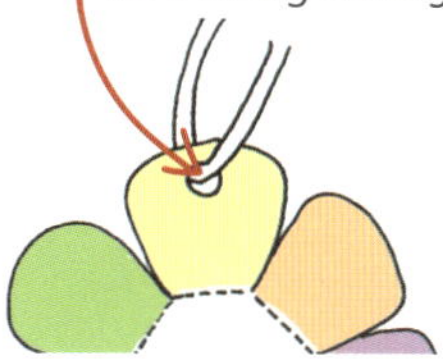

My Works

Awesome Necklace

— CUT
------- FOLD

Fun Activity

My Article

World News

• Business • Finances • Politics • Economics • Sports • Weather •

Draw or write a news story about me 20 years from now!

Awesome person

9 JESUS Always Lives in You

항상 우리와 함께 계셔요

Bible Story — John 14:16-21

When we believe in Jesus we get a new life. He will be with us until the end of the world. He will always protect and help us.

예수님을 믿으면 우리 안에 생명이 생겨요. 예수님은 세상 끝날 때까지 우리와 함께 하세요. 언제나 나를 지켜 주시고 나를 도와주세요.

Memory Verse

Revelation 3:20

Listen! I am standing and knocking at your door. If you hear my voice and open the door, I will come in and we will eat together.

보아라, 내가 문 밖에 서서, 문을 두드리고 있다. 누구든지 내 음성을 듣고 문을 열면, 나는 그에게로 들어가서 그와 함께 먹고, 그는 나와 함께 먹을 것이다. [요한계시록 3:20]

How to Make

WHAT YOU NEED
- coloring tools
- scissors
- glue
- fastener
- hole puncher

❶ Draw yourself and cut out the heart.

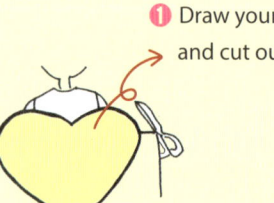

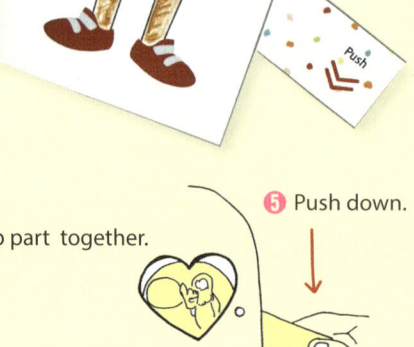

❷ Punch a hole.

❸ Insert the fastener through the hole.

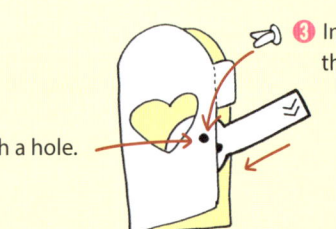

❹ Glue the top part together.

❺ Push down.

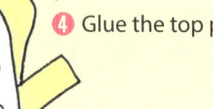

40

Fun Activity

Secret key

Use the code to find the hidden message.
Write the letter for each picture on the line above it.
Read the message aloud.

Answer 56p

43

Sharing SWEET GREAT NEWS

달콤한 복음을 전해요

Do you want to share the love of Jesus to people we care about? The Gospel is good news to anyone!

예수님의 사랑을 내가 좋아하는 사람에게 전할까요? 복음은 누구에게나 기쁜 소식이에요.

"The Lord's Spirit has come to me, because he has chosen me to tell the good news to the poor. The Lord has sent me to announce freedom for prisoners, to give sight to the blind, to free everyone who suffers, and to say, 'This is the year the Lord has chosen.'" [Luke 4:18,19]

"주님의 영이 내게 내리셨다. 주님께서 내게 기름을 부으셔서, 가난한 사람에게 기쁜 소식을 전하게 하셨다. 주님께서 나를 보내셔서, 포로 된 사람들에게 해방을 선포하고, 눈먼 사람들에게 눈 뜸을 선포하고, 억눌린 사람들을 풀어 주고, 주님의 은혜의 해를 선포하게 하셨다." [누가복음 4:18-19]

How to Make

WHAT YOU NEED
scissors
tape
candy or lollipop
pen
craft knife

1. Cut out the circle.
2. fold along the lines.
3. Put the candy in the hole.
4. Glue the top.

1. Make a hole and insert a lollipop.
2. Write the name of the person you want to give it to.
3. Tape the lollipop stick.

My Works

Beloved

I LOVE you so much!

and not powers above or powers below. Nothing in all creation can separate us from God's love for us in Christ Jesus our Lord! _Romans 8:39

© 2022 by kimberly craft All rights reserved

To.

CUT
FOLD

Bless you!

I will bless those who bless you, but I will put a curse on anyone who puts a curse on you. Everyone on earth will be blessed because of you. _Genesis 12:3

© 2022 by kimberly craft All rights reserved

To.

My WORKS
Beloved

--- CUT

To.

Numbers 6:24
I pray that the Lord
will bless and protect you.

To.

Isaiah 41:9
From far across the earth I brought you here and said, "You are my chosen servant. I haven't forgotten you."

To.

Ephesians 4:7
Christ has generously divided out his gifts to us.

To.

Proverbs 4:6
If you love Wisdom and don't reject her, she will watch over you.

Memory Card Matching Game

Cut out the cards.

How to play
1. Mix up the cards.
2. Lay them in rows, face down.
3. Turn over any two cards.
4. If the two cards match, keep them. and go again.
5. If they don't match, turn them back over. Your turn is over.
6. The game is over when all the cards have been matched.
7. Whoever has the most matched pairs, wins!

YOU ARE
awesome

YOU ARE
awesome

YOU ARE
awesome

YOU ARE
awesome

YOU ARE
awesome

YOU ARE
awesome

YOU ARE
awesome

YOU ARE
awesome

YOU ARE
awesome

YOU ARE
awesome

YOU ARE
awesome

YOU ARE
awesome

Love 	God 	Faith 
Gospel 	Cross 	Alive 
Promise 	Salvation 	Jesus 
Life 	Free 	Joy 

YOU ARE
Awesome

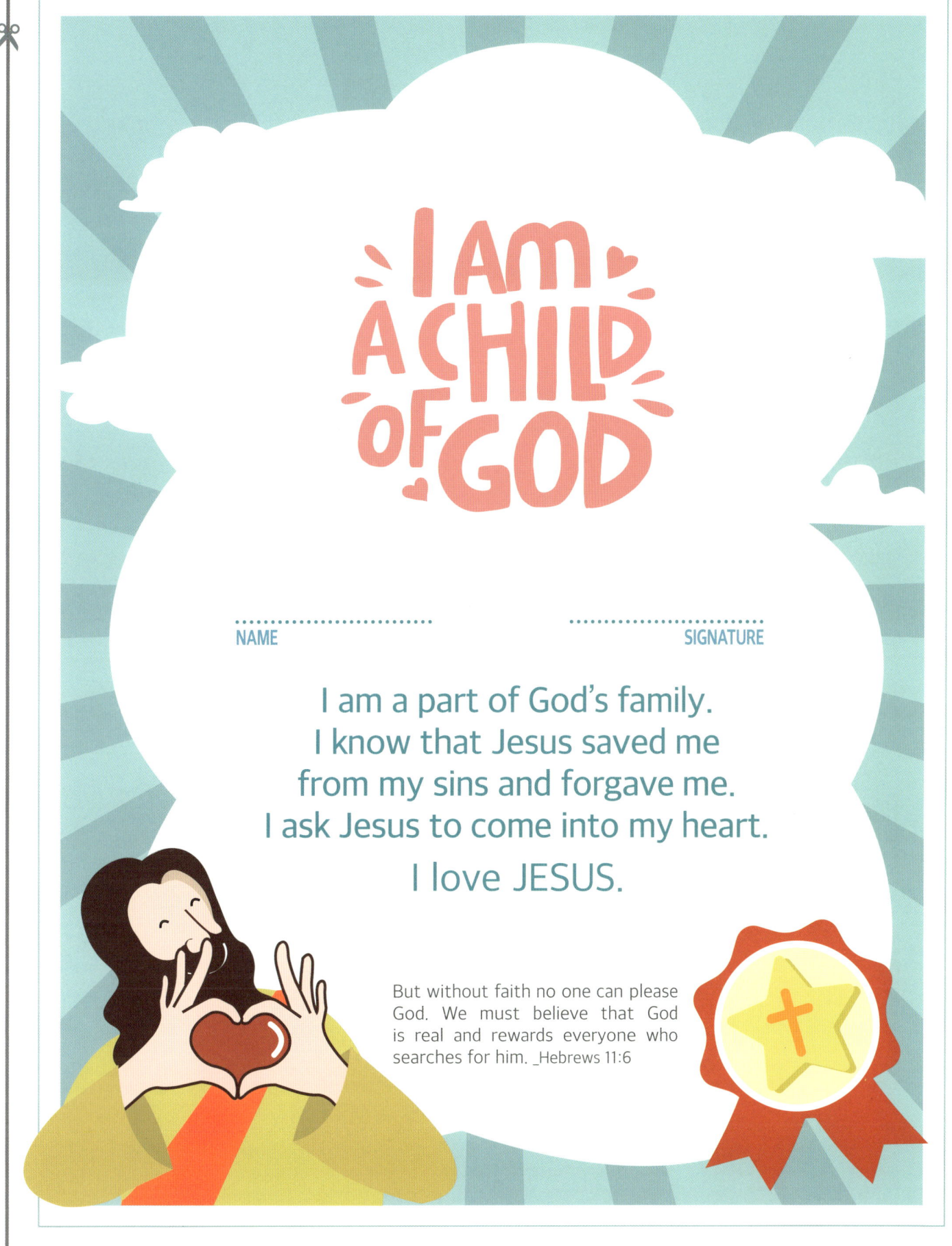

나는 하나님의 가족이 되었습니다. 예수님께서 나의 죄를 용서하시고 구원해 주신 것을 믿습니다. 내 마음에 들어와 주시기를 소망합니다. 예수님 사랑합니다.

믿음이 없이는 하나님을 기쁘게 해드릴 수 없습니다. 하나님께 나아가는 사람은, 하나님이 계시다는 것과, 하나님은 자기를 찾는 사람들에게 상을 주시는 분이시라는 것을 믿어야 합니다. [히브리서 11:6]

Answer

13 page

19 page

23 page

27 page

Answer

31 page

35 page

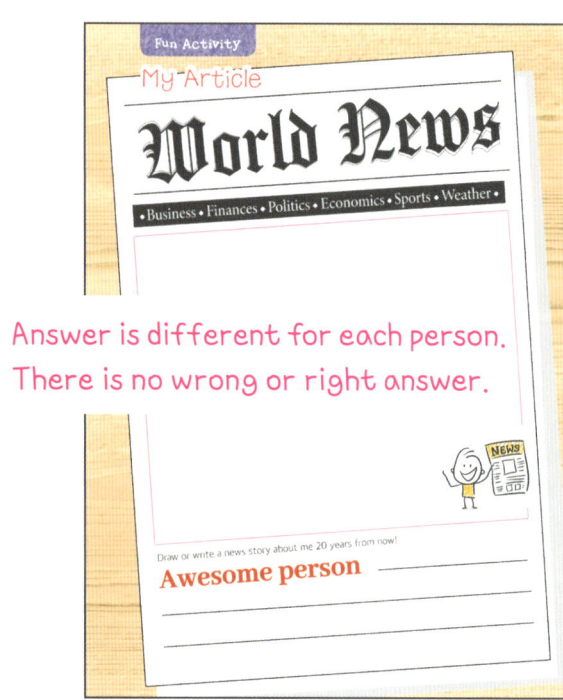

39 page

43 page